Bitcoin

The Revolution of Decentralized Digital Currency and Understanding the Potential, Challenges, and Impact of the World's Most Disruptive Cryptocurrency

Lewis Finan

s

Table of Contents

Introduction

In the realm of finance and technology, few phenomena have captured the world's imagination and stirred as much debate as Bitcoin, the revolutionary decentralized digital currency. Born out of the ashes of the 2008 financial crisis, Bitcoin represents a paradigm shift in the way we perceive and engage with money. Its emergence, shrouded in mystery and pseudonymity, has sparked a global movement towards decentralized financial systems, challenging the traditional notions of currency and economic governance.

"Bitcoin: The Revolution of Decentralized Digital Currency and Understanding the Potential, Challenges, and Impact of the World's Most Disruptive Cryptocurrency" delves into the heart of this groundbreaking innovation, unraveling the intricacies of a digital currency that has become both a symbol of financial freedom and a lightning rod for controversy.

As we embark on this exploration, we will journey through the genesis of Bitcoin, tracing its roots to the visionary pseudonymous creator, Satoshi Nakamoto. We will unravel the cryptographic underpinnings that secure its transactions, exploring the blockchain – a decentralized ledger that forms the backbone of this transformative technology. In doing so, we will demystify the mechanics of Bitcoin, offering clarity to both novices and seasoned enthusiasts alike.

However, this book extends beyond the technical intricacies. It delves into the profound implications of Bitcoin on our global economic landscape, shedding light on its potential to redefine the very nature of money. As governments grapple with the rise of decentralized currencies, we will explore the challenges and regulatory considerations that accompany this paradigm shift.

The journey does not merely focus on the utopian promises of financial liberation; it confronts the complexities and controversies that surround Bitcoin. From its association with illicit activities to the environmental concerns arising from its energy-intensive mining process, we will critically examine the multifaceted nature of this disruptive cryptocurrency.

Moreover, we will scrutinize the broader impact of Bitcoin on financial institutions, investment strategies, and the future of commerce. As Bitcoin's influence extends beyond the digital realm into the mainstream, understanding its potential consequences becomes paramount for individuals, businesses, and policymakers alike.

In these pages, we invite readers to embark on a comprehensive exploration of Bitcoin – from its humble beginnings to its current status as a global financial force. Whether you are a curious observer, a seasoned investor, or someone navigating the complexities of regulatory landscapes, this book aims to provide a holistic understanding of the revolution that is Bitcoin and its enduring impact on our world.

Defining Bitcoin

At its core, Bitcoin is a decentralized digital currency that operates on a peer-to-peer network, enabling direct transactions between users without the need for intermediaries like banks. Conceived in a whitepaper published in 2008 by the elusive figure known as Satoshi Nakamoto, Bitcoin emerged as a response to the shortcomings of traditional financial systems, particularly in the aftermath of the 2008 global financial crisis.

Bitcoin operates on a technology known as blockchain, a distributed and immutable ledger that records all transactions across a network of computers. This technology ensures transparency, security, and decentralization. Unlike traditional currencies issued by governments (fiat currencies), Bitcoin is not controlled by any central authority. Instead, its issuance and transaction verification are managed collectively by a network of participants, known as miners, who use powerful computers to solve complex mathematical problems.

The limited supply of Bitcoin adds to its unique characteristics. There will only ever be 21 million bitcoins in existence, a deliberate design choice by Nakamoto. This scarcity is intended to prevent inflation and mimic the scarcity of precious metals like gold.

Ownership of Bitcoin is established through cryptographic keys. A user's public key serves as their address, visible to others on the network, while the private key, kept secret, is required to access and control the bitcoins associated with that address. This cryptographic security underpins the integrity of the entire Bitcoin network.

Transactions made with Bitcoin are irreversible and, once confirmed by the network, are recorded on the blockchain. The decentralized nature of this ledger ensures resistance to censorship and tampering, making Bitcoin transactions secure and transparent.

Bitcoin has evolved beyond a mere digital currency; it has become a symbol of financial autonomy and an asset class with substantial investment interest. As it continues to challenge conventional notions of money and finance, the definition of Bitcoin extends beyond its technical aspects to encompass a revolutionary force that has the potential to reshape the global economic landscape.

Historical Context of Digital Currency

The historical context of digital currency traces a fascinating journey through the evolution of money and the relentless march of technology.

While the concept of digital currency might seem synonymous with the rise of cryptocurrencies like Bitcoin, its roots delve deeper into the annals of the digital age.

The first glimmers of digital currency experimentation can be found in the mid-20th century when the advent of computers paved the way for innovative financial technologies. In the 1970s, the concept of "digital cash" emerged, largely through the work of renowned cryptographers such as David Chaum. His groundbreaking ideas laid the foundation for the cryptographic protocols that would later inspire modern cryptocurrencies.

The ensuing decades witnessed the rise of electronic payment systems, as financial institutions and businesses sought more efficient and secure ways to conduct transactions. The advent of the internet in the late 20th century further accelerated this trend, with pioneers like DigiCash attempting to create a digital currency for online transactions.

However, these early endeavors faced significant hurdles, including regulatory challenges and issues related to centralization. It wasn't until the publication of the Bitcoin whitepaper in 2008 that a breakthrough occurred, setting the stage for the birth of decentralized digital currencies.

Satoshi Nakamoto's vision for Bitcoin was deeply rooted in a response to the fragilities exposed by the 2008 financial crisis. The pseudonymous creator sought to create a system that would operate without reliance on central authorities, immune to inflationary pressures, and resistant to censorship. The implementation of blockchain technology provided the missing link, offering a decentralized and transparent ledger to record transactions securely.

Bitcoin's launch in 2009 marked a historic moment—the birth of the first decentralized cryptocurrency. Its success sparked a proliferation of alternative cryptocurrencies, collectively known as altcoins, each attempting to address different aspects of the digital currency landscape.

The historical trajectory of digital currency reveals a dynamic interplay between technological innovation, economic exigencies, and societal shifts. As the world becomes increasingly digitized, the evolution of digital currency continues to shape and redefine the landscape of finance, challenging traditional norms and fostering new possibilities for economic interaction on a global scale.

Emergence of Decentralization

The emergence of decentralization represents a transformative shift in various domains, ranging from finance to technology and governance. This paradigm, challenging established centralized models, has roots that extend across different disciplines and historical epochs.

Technological Precursors:

The foundations of decentralization can be traced back to the early days of the Internet. The internet itself is a decentralized network designed to withstand disruptions, with no single point of control. Technologies like peer-to-peer (P2P) file sharing, exemplified by protocols like BitTorrent, hinted at the potential of decentralized systems by allowing direct exchanges between users.

Open Source Movement:

The ethos of decentralization gained momentum with the rise of the open-source software movement. Developers collaborating across the globe on projects like Linux and Apache demonstrated the effectiveness of distributed, community-driven efforts. This model showcased the power of decentralized decision-making and resource sharing.

Cryptocurrency and Blockchain Technology:

The watershed moment for decentralization came with the introduction of Bitcoin in 2009. Satoshi Nakamoto's vision of a decentralized digital currency, powered by blockchain technology, challenged the traditional banking system's reliance on central authorities. Blockchain, a decentralized and tamper-resistant ledger, became the cornerstone of cryptocurrencies, ensuring transparent and secure transactions without intermediaries.

Smart Contracts and Decentralized Applications (DApps):

The evolution continued with the introduction of smart contracts, self-executing agreements with the terms of the contract directly written into code. Ethereum, a blockchain platform that enabled the creation of decentralized applications (DApps), expanded the scope beyond currency. This allowed for the development of decentralized finance (DeFi) applications, further decentralizing financial services.

Decentralized Autonomous Organizations (DAOs):

The concept of DAOs takes decentralization a step further. These are organizations run by code, with decisions made through consensus mechanisms rather than centralized authority. DAOs exemplify the potential for decentralized governance structures, where participants collectively determine the organization's direction.

Data Ownership and Privacy:

Decentralization extends beyond technology to encompass concepts like data ownership and privacy. Decentralized identity solutions and blockchain-based data storage systems empower individuals to control their data, mitigating the risks associated with centralized data repositories.

Political and Social Implications:

The emergence of decentralized systems carries political and social implications. It challenges hierarchical power structures, fostering a more inclusive and equitable distribution of resources. Blockchain-based voting systems, for instance, aim to enhance the transparency and integrity of democratic processes.

In essence, the emergence of decentralization represents a response to the limitations and vulnerabilities of centralized systems. It embodies a vision of a more transparent, inclusive, and resilient future across diverse sectors, reshaping the way we conceive and interact with technology, finance, and governance. As the decentralized paradigm continues to evolve, its impact on various facets of human life promises to be profound and enduring.

Chapter 1: Foundations of Bitcoin

In the turbulent aftermath of the 2008 financial crisis, a pseudonymous figure known as Satoshi Nakamoto introduced the world to a revolutionary concept—Bitcoin. This digital currency, rooted in a desire for financial autonomy and resilience, was underpinned by a set of foundational principles that reshaped the landscape of money and technology.

1. The Genesis: Satoshi Nakamoto's Vision

The story begins with the enigmatic Satoshi Nakamoto, whose whitepaper, titled "Bitcoin: A Peer-to-Peer Electronic Cash System," laid the groundwork for a decentralized digital currency. Nakamoto envisioned a system that would liberate financial transactions from the grip of centralized authorities, fostering trust through cryptographic principles and a peer-to-peer network.

2. Decentralization and the Blockchain Revolution

At the core of Bitcoin's foundations lies the concept of decentralization. Unlike traditional currencies controlled by governments and financial institutions, Bitcoin operates on a decentralized network of computers. The blockchain, a tamper-resistant and transparent ledger, records all transactions, ensuring trust and eliminating the need for intermediaries.

3. Cryptography: Securing the Digital Frontier

The security of Bitcoin relies on cryptographic techniques. Public and private keys, cryptographic hashes, and digital signatures form the intricate web of security measures that safeguard transactions and protect the integrity of the entire network. Understanding these cryptographic principles is essential to grasping the robustness of the Bitcoin ecosystem.

4. Mining: The Backbone of Bitcoin

Bitcoin's issuance and transaction verification are entrusted to a network of miners. These participants use powerful computers to solve complex mathematical puzzles, adding new blocks to the blockchain and validating transactions. The process, known as mining, not only secures the network but also introduces new bitcoins into circulation.

5. Limited Supply: Mimicking Precious Metals

In a deliberate departure from fiat currencies subject to inflation, Nakamoto capped the total supply of bitcoins at 21 million. This scarcity, akin to precious metals like gold, aims to prevent devaluation and create a deflationary economic model. Understanding the implications of this fixed supply is crucial to comprehending Bitcoin's role as a store of value.

6. Evolution of Nodes: Maintaining Consensus

Nodes, the computers participating in the Bitcoin network, play a vital role in maintaining consensus. Full nodes validate and relay transactions, ensuring adherence to the protocol rules. Mining nodes, on the other hand, compete to add new blocks to the blockchain. The intricate interplay of nodes forms the backbone of Bitcoin's decentralized architecture.

As we embark on this exploration of the foundations of Bitcoin, it is essential to grasp these fundamental principles. The genesis of Nakamoto's vision, the power of decentralization, the cryptographic underpinnings, the intricacies of mining, and the economic principles governing Bitcoin lay the groundwork for a deeper understanding of the revolutionary force that is Bitcoin. In the chapters to come, we will unravel the layers of this digital currency, exploring its potential, challenges, and the transformative impact it continues to exert on the world of finance and beyond.

1.1 Blockchain Technology

In the digital age, where trust and transparency are paramount, blockchain technology has emerged as a transformative force, disrupting traditional paradigms across industries. At its essence, a blockchain is a decentralized and distributed ledger that records transactions securely and transparently. Understanding the intricacies of this technology is key to appreciating its wide-ranging applications.

1. Decentralization: The Core Tenet

At the heart of blockchain is the principle of decentralization. Unlike centralized databases controlled by a single authority, a blockchain is maintained by a network of participants, or nodes, distributed across the globe. This decentralized nature ensures that no single entity has control over the entire system, enhancing security and resilience.

2. Immutable and Tamper-Resistant Ledger

The term "blockchain" itself refers to the chain of blocks, where each block contains a list of transactions. Once a block is added to the chain, it is cryptographically linked to the previous block, forming a continuous and unchangeable ledger. The immutability of the blockchain makes it resistant to tampering, providing a high level of trust in the data recorded.

3. Consensus Mechanisms: Ensuring Agreement

To maintain the integrity of the ledger, blockchain networks employ consensus mechanisms. These are protocols that ensure all nodes agree on the validity of transactions. Common consensus mechanisms include Proof of Work (used by Bitcoin) and Proof of Stake. These mechanisms prevent malicious actors from altering the blockchain and maintain the network's trustworthiness.

4. Smart Contracts: Self-Executing Code

Smart contracts are self-executing contracts with the terms directly written into code. These contracts automatically execute and enforce the agreed-upon terms when predefined conditions are met. Ethereum, a prominent blockchain platform, popularized smart contracts, enabling the creation of decentralized applications (DApps) that operate without intermediaries.

5. Transparent and Pseudonymous Transactions

Blockchain transactions are transparent and traceable. Anyone can view the entire transaction history, promoting accountability. However, users are pseudonymous, identified by cryptographic addresses rather than personal information. This privacy feature offers a balance between transparency and user confidentiality.

6. Tokenization: Digital Assets on Blockchain

Blockchain facilitates the creation of digital assets through a process called tokenization. These tokens represent ownership or access rights and can represent various assets, including real estate, art, or even shares in a company. Tokenization has the potential to democratize access to assets and redefine ownership models.

7. Cross-Border Transactions and Interoperability

Blockchain technology has the potential to streamline cross-border transactions by eliminating intermediaries and reducing transaction times. Additionally, efforts are underway to enhance interoperability between different blockchain networks, allowing them to communicate and share information seamlessly.

As blockchain technology continues to evolve, its impact spans diverse industries, from finance and supply chain to healthcare and beyond. The decentralized, secure, and transparent nature of blockchain has the potential to reshape how we transact, share information, and establish trust in the digital era. Exploring its applications and understanding its potential challenges are essential steps in navigating the transformative landscape of blockchain technology.

1.2 Cryptography in Bitcoin

Bitcoin, the pioneering decentralized digital currency, relies fundamentally on cryptographic principles to secure transactions, ensure the integrity of the network, and provide users with a level of privacy and control unparalleled in traditional financial systems. Understanding the role of cryptography in Bitcoin is essential for grasping the robust security measures that underpin this groundbreaking technology.

1. Public and Private Keys: The Foundation of Ownership

At the core of Bitcoin's cryptographic security are public and private key pairs. A public key serves as an address to which others can send bitcoins, while the corresponding private key is kept confidential and is used to access and control the bitcoins associated with that address. The strength of this cryptographic pairing lies in the computational difficulty of deriving the private key from the public key.

2. Digital Signatures: Verifying Authenticity

Digital signatures play a pivotal role in ensuring the authenticity and integrity of Bitcoin transactions. When a user initiates a transaction, their private key is used to create a digital signature. This signature, when verified with the user's public key, confirms the transaction's legitimacy. The decentralized nature of the Bitcoin network relies on these digital signatures to prevent fraudulent activities.

3. Hash Functions: Creating Immutable Records

Bitcoin uses cryptographic hash functions to create a unique and fixed-size representation of data. Each block in the blockchain contains a cryptographic hash of the previous block, forming a chain. This interconnection makes altering any block infeasible without changing all subsequent blocks, ensuring the immutability of the transaction history.

4. Proof of Work: Mining for Security

The Proof of Work (PoW) consensus algorithm, a cryptographic puzzle-solving process, is integral to Bitcoin's security. Miners compete to solve complex mathematical problems, with the first to solve it adding a new block to the blockchain. This process not only secures the network but also introduces new bitcoins into circulation. PoW ensures that the creation of new blocks is resource-intensive, adding a layer of security against malicious actors.

5. Elliptic Curve Cryptography: Efficient Security

Bitcoin employs elliptic curve cryptography (ECC) for its key pairs, striking a balance between security and computational efficiency. ECC provides a level of security comparable to traditional cryptographic systems but with shorter key lengths, reducing the computational load on the network and making transactions more efficient.

6. Hierarchical Deterministic Wallets: Enhancing Privacy

Hierarchical Deterministic (HD) wallets in Bitcoin use mathematical algorithms to generate a sequence of key pairs from a single seed. This not only streamlines the process of creating and managing multiple addresses but also enhances user privacy by preventing address reuse, a crucial factor in maintaining confidentiality.

7. Securing the Network: Cryptographic Resilience

Cryptography in Bitcoin extends beyond individual transactions; it forms the backbone of the entire network's security. The robustness of cryptographic algorithms ensures that the decentralized nature of Bitcoin remains resilient against various potential attacks.

In summary, the cryptographic foundations of Bitcoin are integral to its security, privacy, and decentralized nature. From key pairs and digital signatures to hash functions and Proof of Work, these cryptographic mechanisms collectively contribute to making Bitcoin a groundbreaking and secure digital currency, challenging conventional notions of trust and financial transactions.

1.3 Mining and the Proof-of-Work Concept

Bitcoin's unique consensus algorithm, known as Proof of Work (PoW), is the driving force behind the process known as mining. Mining is not just a technical term; it represents a fundamental aspect of how new bitcoins are created, transactions are verified, and the security of the entire Bitcoin network is maintained. Understanding the intricacies of mining and the Proof-of-Work concept is crucial for comprehending the decentralized nature of Bitcoin.

1. Mining: Unearthing New Bitcoins

Mining is the process by which new bitcoins are introduced into circulation, and it involves solving complex mathematical puzzles. Miners, individuals, or groups of individuals with specialized hardware, compete to solve these puzzles. The first miner to solve the puzzle gets the privilege of adding a new block to the blockchain and is rewarded with a predetermined amount of newly minted bitcoins, along with transaction fees from the transactions included in the block.

2. Proof of Work: Ensuring Security

Proof of Work is the consensus mechanism that underlies the mining process. It is a cryptographic puzzle that miners must solve to add a new block to the blockchain. The difficulty of the puzzle is dynamically adjusted by the network to ensure that, on average, a new block is added approximately every 10 minutes. This feature is crucial for maintaining a predictable issuance of new bitcoins and preventing the blockchain from becoming cluttered with transactions.

3. Solving the Puzzle: Computational Competition

The PoW puzzle requires miners to find a specific value (known as a nonce) that, when hashed with the contents of the block, produces a hash that meets certain criteria (usually starting with a certain number of leading zeros). Since hashing is a one-way function, miners must perform numerous calculations through trial and error until they find the correct nonce that satisfies the puzzle conditions.

4. Competition and Consensus: Incentivizing Honest Participation

The competitive nature of mining serves as a safeguard against malicious actors. To successfully alter a block in the blockchain, an attacker would need to redo the Proof-of-Work for that block and all subsequent blocks, which becomes computationally infeasible as more blocks are added over time. This consensus mechanism ensures that the majority of participants in the network are honest and that the blockchain remains secure.

5. Mining Pools: Collaborative Mining

Mining has become highly competitive and resource-intensive, leading to the formation of mining pools. In a mining pool, individual miners combine their computational power to increase their chances of successfully solving a block and earning the associated rewards. Once a block is successfully mined, the rewards are distributed among the pool members based on their contributed computational power.

6. Energy Consumption Debate: Environmental Considerations

One of the ongoing debates surrounding Bitcoin mining is its energy consumption. The computational power required to solve PoW puzzles demands significant electricity. While this has led to concerns about the environmental impact, proponents argue that this energy expenditure is a critical aspect of maintaining the security and decentralization of the network.

In summary, mining and the Proof-of-Work concept are integral to the functioning of the Bitcoin network. Mining not only creates new bitcoins but also ensures the security and decentralization of the blockchain through a competitive and computationally intensive process. As the Bitcoin ecosystem evolves, ongoing discussions about the environmental impact and potential alternative consensus mechanisms continue to shape the future of mining in the world of cryptocurrencies.

Chapter 2: The Bitcoin Ecosystem

In the dynamic landscape of digital currencies, Bitcoin stands as a pioneer, shaping an ecosystem that extends far beyond its initial conception. This chapter delves into the multifaceted elements that constitute the Bitcoin ecosystem, exploring the diverse actors, technologies, and applications that contribute to its vibrancy.

1. Nodes and Network Architecture

At the heart of the Bitcoin ecosystem are nodes—computers that participate in the decentralized network. Full nodes validate and relay transactions, ensuring adherence to the rules of the Bitcoin protocol. Mining nodes, equipped with powerful hardware, engage in the Proof-of-Work process to add new blocks to the blockchain. The collective interaction of nodes establishes the robust architecture that underpins the entire Bitcoin network.

2. Wallets: Gateways to Bitcoin Ownership

Bitcoin wallets play a pivotal role as the interface between users and the blockchain. These wallets, ranging from software applications to hardware devices, enable individuals to store, send, and receive bitcoins. Understanding the nuances of wallet security, from hot wallets connected to the internet to cold wallets kept offline, is essential for users navigating the intricacies of Bitcoin ownership.

3. Exchanges: Facilitating Bitcoin Trading

Exchanges form the bustling marketplaces where users buy and sell bitcoins. These platforms provide liquidity, price discovery, and accessibility to a global user base. As key intermediaries, exchanges also introduce considerations of security, regulation, and the evolving landscape of cryptocurrency markets.

4. Developers and Innovation

The Bitcoin ecosystem thrives on innovation driven by developers. Open-source contributions and improvements to the Bitcoin codebase enhance the network's functionality and security. Beyond Bitcoin's core protocol, developers explore and create layers of innovation, from second-layer scaling solutions like the Lightning Network to novel applications and smart contracts.

5. Regulatory Landscape

As Bitcoin gains prominence, the regulatory landscape evolves in tandem. Governments and regulatory bodies grapple with defining frameworks that balance innovation and security. Understanding the diverse approaches globally is essential for participants in the Bitcoin ecosystem, from users and developers to businesses and financial institutions.

6. Adoption and Mainstream Integration

Bitcoin's journey from a niche concept to mainstream adoption is marked by increasing acceptance in various sectors. From merchants and service providers accepting Bitcoin payments to institutional investment, the integration of Bitcoin into traditional financial systems marks a transformative shift in the global economic landscape.

7. Challenges and Debates

The Bitcoin ecosystem is not devoid of challenges and debates. Scalability concerns, environmental impacts of mining, and ongoing discussions about the role of privacy in transactions underscore the complexities inherent in this rapidly evolving space. Exploring these debates provides insights into the resilience and adaptability of the Bitcoin ecosystem.

8. Social and Cultural Impact

Beyond the technical aspects, Bitcoin has a profound social and cultural impact. It symbolizes financial autonomy, challenges traditional notions of money, and sparks conversations about economic inclusivity. Understanding these broader implications contributes to a holistic comprehension of the role Bitcoin plays in shaping societal narratives.

As we navigate the diverse components of the Bitcoin ecosystem in this chapter, it becomes evident that Bitcoin's significance extends far beyond its role as a digital currency. It is a dynamic and evolving ecosystem, shaped by a diverse array of actors and factors, contributing to the ongoing narrative of decentralization, innovation, and the reimagining of global finance. In the subsequent chapters, we will delve deeper into specific aspects of this ecosystem, exploring the implications, challenges, and potential trajectories that define the world of Bitcoin.

2.1 Wallets and Exchanges

Wallets: Safeguarding Your Digital Wealth

Bitcoin ownership begins with a wallet—a digital tool that allows users to store, manage, and transact with their bitcoins. Wallets come in various forms, each catering to different needs and preferences.

1. Hot Wallets: Connected Convenience

Hot wallets are online wallets accessible through web browsers or mobile apps. They provide convenience for everyday transactions but are connected to the internet, making them susceptible to cyber threats. Users often use hot wallets for small, regularly conducted transactions.

2. Cold Wallets: Offline Security

Cold wallets, in contrast, are offline storage solutions, adding an extra layer of security. Hardware wallets, paper wallets, and even air-gapped computers fall into this category. By keeping private keys offline, cold wallets mitigate the risk of online hacking, making them ideal for long-term storage.

3. Software Wallets: Balancing Accessibility and Security

Software wallets include desktop, mobile, and web wallets. While they offer accessibility, users should choose reputable providers and prioritize security practices like two-factor authentication. Software wallets cater to a broad range of users, from beginners to advanced enthusiasts.

4. Multisignature Wallets: Shared Control

Multisignature wallets require multiple private keys to authorize a Bitcoin transaction. This feature enhances security by distributing control among different parties. It's commonly used for joint accounts, providing added protection against unauthorized access.

Exchanges: Bridging the Fiat-Crypto Gap

Bitcoin exchanges serve as vital gateways, enabling users to convert fiat currency into bitcoin and vice versa. These platforms facilitate price discovery, liquidity, and the opportunity to trade bitcoin as a financial asset.

1. Centralized Exchanges: Liquidity Hubs

Centralized exchanges (CEX) are platforms that act as intermediaries, matching buyers with sellers. They offer high liquidity and a wide range of trading pairs. However, users must trust the exchange with their funds, and security breaches, though rare, can have significant consequences.

2. Decentralized Exchanges: Empowering Users

Decentralized exchanges (DEX) operate without a central authority, allowing users to trade directly from their wallets. This model aligns with the ethos of decentralization but may face challenges related to liquidity and user experience.

3. Peer-to-Peer Platforms: Direct Transactions

Peer-to-peer (P2P) platforms connect buyers and sellers directly. These platforms often incorporate an escrow service to ensure a secure transaction. P2P trading provides users with more control but demands a level of caution and due diligence.

4. Over-the-Counter (OTC) Trading: Institutional Solutions

OTC trading caters to institutional investors and high-net-worth individuals. It involves direct, off-exchange trading, often in large volumes. OTC desks offer privacy, personalized services, and reduced impact on the market.

Considerations for Users

1. Security: Safeguarding Your Assets

Security is paramount. Users should prioritize wallets and exchanges with robust security features, including encryption, two-factor authentication, and cold storage solutions for significant holdings.

2. Usability: Tailoring to Your Needs

The choice between wallets and exchanges should align with individual needs. Frequent traders may prioritize the user experience of an exchange, while long-term investors might favor the security features of specific wallet types.

3. Regulatory Compliance: Navigating Legal Frameworks

Users should be aware of the regulatory landscape governing wallets and exchanges in their jurisdiction. Complying with legal requirements ensures a smooth and lawful experience in the Bitcoin ecosystem.

4. Reputation and Reviews: Informed Decision-Making

Researching and choosing reputable wallets and exchanges is crucial. User reviews, industry reputation, and the track record of security incidents can guide users in making informed decisions.

In the dynamic realm of Bitcoin, wallets and exchanges serve as essential tools, each playing a distinct role in the user experience. Whether securing digital wealth or navigating the complexities of the market, understanding the nuances of wallets and exchanges empowers users to engage confidently in the world of cryptocurrencies.

2.2 Smart Contracts and Decentralized Applications

The advent of blockchain technology has ushered in not only a new form of currency, like Bitcoin, but also a broader spectrum of possibilities. Among these, smart contracts and decentralized applications (DApps) stand out, representing the evolution of decentralized, trustless, and programmable systems.

Smart Contracts: Self-Executing Code

Smart contracts are self-executing contracts with the terms directly written into code. Developed on blockchain platforms like Ethereum, these contracts automatically enforce and execute the agreed-upon terms when predefined conditions are met. The introduction of smart contracts revolutionizes the way agreements are made, removing the need for intermediaries and providing transparency and security.

1. Code as Law: Enforcing Agreements

The code within a smart contract is immutable and runs on the blockchain. This concept gives rise to the phrase "code is law," as the execution of the contract is automatic and irreversible once triggered.

This feature ensures trust and eliminates the reliance on a central authority for contract enforcement.

2. Use Cases: Beyond Currency Transactions

While Bitcoin primarily focuses on peer-to-peer transactions, smart contracts extend blockchain functionality to a broader array of use cases. They can be employed in areas such as legal agreements, real estate transactions, supply chain management, and even crowdfunding. The versatility of smart contracts allows for a wide range of decentralized applications.

3. Decentralized Autonomous Organizations (DAOs): Community Governance

DAOs are entities governed by smart contracts, where decisions are made collectively based on consensus mechanisms. Members, often represented by tokens, vote on proposals, and the outcomes are automatically implemented through smart contracts. DAOs exemplify the potential for decentralized and community-driven governance structures.

Decentralized Applications (DApps): Building on Blockchain

Decentralized applications, or DApps, leverage blockchain technology to function without reliance on a central authority. Built on blockchain platforms like Ethereum, EOS, or Binance Smart Chain, DApps aims to provide secure, transparent, and tamper-resistant alternatives to traditional centralized applications.

1. Open Source Development: Collaborative Innovation

DApps often follow the principles of open-source development, allowing anyone to view, modify, and contribute to their source code. This collaborative approach fosters innovation, community engagement, and the continuous improvement of DApp functionalities.

2. Tokenization: Incentivizing Participation

Many DApps incorporate tokens as a means of incentivizing user participation. These tokens often serve multiple purposes, such as granting access to specific features, participating in governance decisions, or representing ownership of digital assets within the application.

3. Decentralized Finance (DeFi): Transforming Finance

A significant sector within the DApp ecosystem is decentralized finance or DeFi. DeFi platforms utilize smart contracts to recreate traditional financial services such as lending, borrowing, trading, and yield farming in a decentralized manner. DeFi represents a paradigm shift in the financial landscape, offering increased accessibility and reducing reliance on centralized intermediaries.

4. Gaming and Non-Fungible Tokens (NFTs): Digital Assets on the Blockchain

DApps are prevalent in the gaming industry, where blockchain provides ownership and provenance for in-game assets. Non-fungible tokens (NFTs) represent unique digital or physical items and have gained popularity in the realm of digital art, collectibles, and gaming.

Challenges and Future Directions

While smart contracts and DApps hold immense promise, challenges persist. Scalability, interoperability between different blockchains, and ensuring security in the ever-evolving landscape of decentralized technologies are areas that demand continuous attention. As blockchain ecosystems mature, ongoing innovations and solutions seek to address these challenges, paving the way for the broader adoption of smart contracts and decentralized applications. The future holds the promise of a decentralized digital landscape where trust, transparency, and programmability redefine how we interact with applications and agreements.

2.3 Regulatory Landscape

The regulatory landscape surrounding cryptocurrencies is a dynamic and evolving domain that varies significantly across different jurisdictions. Governments and regulatory bodies worldwide are grappling with the challenge of striking a balance between fostering innovation and protecting consumers, investors, and the broader financial system. Here, we explore key aspects of the regulatory environment for cryptocurrencies.

1. Global Variances: Divergent Approaches

Cryptocurrency regulations vary widely across countries, with some embracing these digital assets, others cautiously navigating their integration and some imposing outright bans. The lack of a unified global approach results in a complex patchwork of regulations, creating challenges for businesses and users operating in the international cryptocurrency space.

2. Classification: Commodity, Currency, or Security?

One of the fundamental regulatory challenges is determining how to classify cryptocurrencies. Different jurisdictions categorize them in various ways: as commodities, currencies, securities, or a hybrid of these classifications. The classification has significant implications for the applicable regulations, tax treatment, and compliance requirements.

3. AML/KYC Compliance: Combating Illicit Activities

Anti-Money Laundering (AML) and Know Your Customer (KYC) regulations are central components of cryptocurrency regulatory frameworks. Governments aim to mitigate the risks of illicit activities, such as money laundering and terrorist financing, by imposing stringent identity verification and transaction monitoring requirements on cryptocurrency exchanges and service providers.

4. Taxation: Clarifying Obligations

Taxation of cryptocurrencies remains a complex and evolving area. Different jurisdictions apply varied tax treatments, including capital gains taxes, income taxes, or a combination of both. Clear guidance on how to report and calculate taxes on cryptocurrency transactions is essential for users and businesses to comply with local tax laws.

5. Consumer Protection: Safeguarding Investors

Regulators are increasingly focusing on protecting cryptocurrency investors and consumers. Measures include disclosure requirements, risk warnings, and regulations to ensure fair and transparent trading practices. Some jurisdictions have established investor education initiatives to enhance public understanding of the risks associated with cryptocurrency investments.

6. Securities Regulation: ICOs and Token Offerings

Initial Coin Offerings (ICOs) and token offerings have been a focal point of regulatory scrutiny. Authorities in various countries assess whether tokens offered in these fundraising activities qualify as securities, subjecting them to existing securities regulations. This scrutiny aims to protect investors and maintain the integrity of capital markets.

7. **Central Bank Digital Currencies (CBDCs): A Regulatory Frontier**

As central banks explore the issuance of their digital currencies, the regulatory landscape is poised for further transformation. The potential integration of Central Bank Digital Currencies (CBDCs) introduces new considerations related to monetary policy, financial stability, and the overall structure of the financial system.

8. **Blockchain and Smart Contracts: Legal Recognition**

While regulators focus on cryptocurrencies, the underlying blockchain technology and smart contracts also pose legal questions. Some jurisdictions are working to provide legal recognition and clarity around the enforceability of smart contracts, paving the way for broader adoption of blockchain-based solutions.

9. **International Cooperation: Addressing Challenges Together**

Given the borderless nature of cryptocurrencies, there is an increasing recognition of the need for international cooperation. Forums and organizations, such as the Financial Action Task Force (FATF), aim to establish global standards and facilitate collaboration among regulators to address common challenges.

10. Ongoing Evolution: Navigating Uncertainty

The regulatory landscape for cryptocurrencies is in a state of continual evolution. Ongoing developments, including court decisions, regulatory updates, and industry collaborations, contribute to the ongoing refinement of the regulatory framework. Participants in the cryptocurrency space must remain vigilant and adaptable to navigate this dynamic environment.

In conclusion, the regulatory landscape for cryptocurrencies is characterized by its diversity, complexity, and ongoing evolution. As governments and regulatory bodies continue to grapple with the challenges posed by digital assets, stakeholders in the cryptocurrency ecosystem must stay informed, engage with regulators, and actively contribute to the shaping of a regulatory framework that fosters innovation while ensuring the protection of users and the broader financial system.

Chapter 3: Potential of Bitcoin

In the ever-evolving landscape of finance and technology, Bitcoin has emerged as a disruptive force with the potential to redefine traditional notions of currency, value transfer, and financial sovereignty. This chapter explores the multifaceted potential of Bitcoin, examining its impact on various aspects of the global economy, finance, and beyond.

1.   Store of Value: Digital Gold

Bitcoin's most widely recognized potential lies in its capacity to serve as a store of value often referred to as "digital gold." With a capped supply of 21 million coins, Bitcoin's scarcity mirrors precious metals like gold. This characteristic positions Bitcoin as a hedge against inflation and economic uncertainties, attracting investors seeking a reliable store of wealth.

2.   Decentralization: Redefining Authority

At the core of Bitcoin's potential is its decentralized nature. Operating on a peer-to-peer network without reliance on central authorities, Bitcoin challenges the traditional financial system's hierarchical structures. This decentralization not only enhances security but also fosters financial inclusivity, providing access to individuals in regions with limited banking infrastructure.

3.   Financial Inclusion: Empowering the Unbanked

Bitcoin has the potential to bridge gaps in financial inclusion by providing individuals without access to traditional banking systems with an alternative means of participating in the global economy. Through the use of Bitcoin wallets on mobile devices, people in underserved regions can engage in financial transactions and store value independently.

4.   Remittances: Streamlining Cross-Border Transactions

The borderless nature of Bitcoin enables efficient and cost-effective cross-border transactions. For individuals in regions reliant on remittances, Bitcoin offers a faster and more affordable alternative to traditional remittance channels. This potential has the capacity to disrupt the remittance industry and reduce the financial burden on migrant workers.

5.   Programmable Money: Smart Contracts and Beyond

Bitcoin's programmability extends beyond simple transactions. While not as inherently flexible as platforms like Ethereum, Bitcoin's scripting language allows for the creation of basic smart contracts. The potential for more sophisticated applications is a subject of ongoing development and exploration within the Bitcoin community.

6.   Security and Trust: Immutable Transactions

The use of blockchain technology ensures the immutability and transparency of transactions. This inherent security feature, coupled with the decentralized consensus mechanism, enhances trust in the Bitcoin network. As a result, Bitcoin has the potential to provide a secure and transparent alternative to traditional financial systems.

7.   Monetary Policy Innovation: Fixed Supply

Bitcoin's fixed supply, capped at 21 million coins, represents a departure from traditional fiat currencies subject to inflationary pressures. This deflationary economic model, embedded in Bitcoin's protocol, introduces a novel approach to monetary policy. The potential implications of this innovation continue to fuel discussions about the future of global finance.

8.   Economic Sovereignty: Individual Empowerment

Bitcoin empowers individuals with a level of economic sovereignty that transcends geographical and political boundaries. Through ownership of private keys, users have direct control over their funds, reducing reliance on traditional banking institutions and asserting a form of financial autonomy.

9.   Challenges and Considerations: Scalability and Adoption

While Bitcoin holds significant potential, challenges such as scalability, energy consumption concerns, and regulatory uncertainties loom. Scalability solutions, ongoing technological innovations, and collaborative efforts within the Bitcoin community aim to address these challenges and unlock the full potential of the network.

10. The Future Trajectory: Evolving Narratives

The potential of Bitcoin is a narrative in continuous evolution. As it intersects with technological advancements, societal changes, and regulatory developments, the trajectory of Bitcoin's impact on the world remains dynamic. Stakeholders, from developers and investors to policymakers and the broader public, contribute to shaping the future narrative of Bitcoin's potential.

In the chapters to come, we will delve deeper into specific dimensions of Bitcoin's potential, exploring the challenges, debates, and ongoing innovations that define its role in the global financial landscape. Bitcoin's journey is not only a technological phenomenon but a socio-economic paradigm shift with implications that extend far beyond the realm of digital currencies.

3.1 Economic Implications

Bitcoin, as a decentralized digital currency and store of value, has profound economic implications that ripple through traditional financial systems, global commerce, and the broader economic landscape. This section explores key economic aspects influenced by the adoption and integration of Bitcoin.

1.   Currency Evolution: Redefining Money

Bitcoin challenges traditional notions of currency, serving as a decentralized and borderless alternative. Its fixed supply and resistance to inflation make it a unique store of value, prompting discussions about the future of money and the coexistence of digital currencies with traditional fiat.

2.   Financial Inclusion: Bridging Gaps

In regions with limited banking infrastructure, Bitcoin's decentralized nature provides a pathway to financial inclusion. Unbanked and underbanked populations can access financial services, engage in global trade, and store wealth without dependence on traditional banking institutions.

3.   Remittances: Disrupting Traditional Channels

Bitcoin's efficiency in cross-border transactions has the potential to disrupt traditional remittance channels. Migrant workers can send funds faster and at lower costs, reducing the financial burden on both senders and recipients.

4. Monetary Policy Paradigm: Deflationary Model

Bitcoin's capped supply challenges the conventional monetary policy paradigm. With a fixed maximum of 21 million coins, Bitcoin introduces a deflationary economic model that contrasts with the inflationary nature of traditional fiat currencies. This shift prompts discussions about the long-term impact on economic dynamics.

5. Macro-economic Stability: Decentralized Resilience

The decentralized nature of Bitcoin contributes to macroeconomic stability. Unlike centralized systems susceptible to political and economic upheavals, Bitcoin operates independently, providing an alternative that can thrive amidst global uncertainties.

6. Hedging Against Inflation: Digital Gold

Bitcoin's narrative as "digital gold" positions it as a hedge against inflation. Investors and institutions increasingly view Bitcoin as a store of value comparable to precious metals, seeking protection from currency devaluation and economic uncertainties.

7. Smart Contracts and Business Innovation

The programmability of Bitcoin through smart contracts opens avenues for innovative business applications. From streamlining complex transactions to enabling decentralized finance (DeFi) applications, the potential for business innovation on the Bitcoin blockchain is a dynamic frontier.

8. Energy Consumption Debate: Environmental Considerations

The energy consumption associated with Bitcoin mining has sparked debates about its environmental impact. Balancing the potential economic benefits of Bitcoin with sustainability considerations remains a focal point in discussions about its long-term viability.

9. Regulatory Dynamics: Shaping the Landscape

Bitcoin's economic implications are significantly influenced by regulatory decisions. Clear and supportive regulations can foster innovation and broader adoption, while uncertain or restrictive regulatory environments may impede the growth and integration of Bitcoin into traditional financial systems.

10. Market Dynamics: New Asset Class

Bitcoin has evolved into a distinct asset class, influencing traditional financial markets. Institutional adoption, Bitcoin futures, and the emergence of cryptocurrency exchanges contribute to a shifting landscape where Bitcoin plays a role alongside traditional investments.

11. Global Trade and Commerce: Borderless Transactions

Bitcoin facilitates borderless transactions, simplifying international trade and commerce. Businesses can engage in transactions without the constraints of traditional banking hours, currency conversions, or delays associated with intermediary banks.

12. Wealth Redistribution and Empowerment

Bitcoin's decentralized nature allows for wealth redistribution and individual empowerment. It provides opportunities for individuals to control their finances, reducing dependence on centralized financial institutions and fostering economic empowerment at the individual level.

In conclusion, the economic implications of Bitcoin are far-reaching, touching on currency dynamics, financial inclusion, macroeconomic stability, and the evolving landscape of global trade. As Bitcoin continues to mature, its economic impact will shape and be shaped by ongoing technological advancements, regulatory developments, and societal acceptance, influencing the broader economic narrative in the years to come.

3.2 Financial Inclusion

Financial inclusion, the accessibility, and availability of financial services to all segments of society, is a global challenge with significant implications for economic development. Bitcoin, as a decentralized digital currency, presents a transformative potential in addressing barriers to financial inclusion.

1. **Global Accessibility: Beyond Traditional Banking**

Bitcoin operates on a decentralized network, enabling users to access financial services independent of traditional banking infrastructure. This is particularly impactful in regions where physical banks are scarce or inaccessible, providing a borderless solution for the unbanked and underbanked.

2. **Low-Cost Transactions: Reducing Remittance Costs**

Bitcoin's borderless nature allows for cost-effective cross-border transactions. For individuals relying on remittances, Bitcoin offers a faster and more economical alternative to traditional remittance channels. Reduced transaction costs contribute to increased financial resources for both senders and recipients.

3. **Financial Sovereignty: Individual Empowerment**

Bitcoin provides individuals with direct control over their finances. Through ownership of private keys, users become their own custodians, reducing dependence on centralized financial institutions. This level of financial sovereignty empowers individuals to manage their funds securely and independently.

4. **Microtransactions: Empowering Small Businesses**

Bitcoin facilitates microtransactions, enabling small businesses and entrepreneurs to engage in economic activities that might be hindered by high transaction fees in traditional financial systems. This inclusivity supports the growth of local economies and contributes to poverty alleviation.

5.   Banking the Unbanked: Overcoming Barriers

The decentralized nature of Bitcoin allows individuals without traditional forms of identification or credit history to participate in financial transactions. This inclusivity can be instrumental in bringing marginalized populations into the financial ecosystem, allowing them to build financial identities.

6.   Educational Opportunities: Financial Literacy

Bitcoin's simplicity and accessibility can serve as a tool for financial education. By providing individuals with the means to access and use digital currencies, Bitcoin can contribute to enhanced financial literacy, empowering users to make informed financial decisions.

7.   Decentralized Finance (DeFi): Democratizing Services

The emergence of decentralized finance (DeFi) applications on the Bitcoin blockchain further expands financial inclusion. These applications offer services such as lending, borrowing, and earning interest without the need for traditional intermediaries, making financial services more widely available.

8. Savings and Investments: Wealth Creation

Bitcoin provides a means for individuals to save and invest, potentially generating wealth over time. This is particularly significant in regions where traditional savings options may be limited, offering an alternative avenue for individuals to participate in wealth creation.

9. Community Empowerment: Peer-to-Peer Transactions

Bitcoin's peer-to-peer nature facilitates direct transactions between individuals. This is especially impactful in close-knit communities, enabling community members to transact with one another without the need for intermediaries or reliance on centralized financial institutions.

10. Mobile Banking Solutions: Accessibility on Devices

The use of Bitcoin wallets on mobile devices enhances accessibility. With the prevalence of smartphones even in remote areas, individuals can engage in financial transactions, access savings, and participate in the global economy using just a mobile device and an internet connection.

11. Philanthropy and Aid: Direct Contributions

Bitcoin has been employed in philanthropy and aid efforts, allowing for direct contributions to individuals in need. By bypassing traditional channels, Bitcoin ensures that a larger portion of donations reaches the intended recipients, contributing to more effective aid distribution.

In conclusion, Bitcoin's role in fostering financial inclusion is multifaceted, offering solutions to the unbanked and underbanked, reducing transaction costs, and empowering individuals with greater control over their finances. As Bitcoin continues to evolve, its potential to contribute to global financial inclusion remains a powerful driver for positive economic change.

3.3 Global Impact of Bitcoin on Traditional Banking

Bitcoin, as a decentralized digital currency, has ushered in a paradigm shift in the global financial landscape, influencing traditional banking systems in various ways. This section explores the impact of Bitcoin on traditional banking and the evolving dynamics between the two.

1. Decentralization Challenge: Redefining Authority

Bitcoin challenges the centralized authority of traditional banking systems. Operating on a decentralized blockchain, Bitcoin transactions occur directly between users, reducing the need for intermediaries. This decentralization challenges the traditional banking model where banks serve as intermediaries in financial transactions.

2.   Borderless Transactions: Overcoming Geographical Barriers

Bitcoin's borderless nature facilitates cross-border transactions without the need for traditional banking infrastructure. This challenges the traditional banking notion of geographical constraints, allowing individuals to engage in global transactions without relying on correspondent banks and international wire transfer systems.

3.   Financial Inclusion: Bridging Gaps

Bitcoin's accessibility extends financial services to the unbanked and underbanked populations, challenging the exclusivity of traditional banking. Individuals without access to traditional banking infrastructure can participate in the global economy, transact, and store value through Bitcoin wallets on their mobile devices.

4.   Reduced Intermediation: Disintermediation Potential

Bitcoin's peer-to-peer nature reduces the reliance on traditional banking intermediaries. While traditional banks provide a range of financial services, Bitcoin's emergence has the potential to disintermediate certain transactions, particularly those involving cross-border payments and remittances.

5.   Digital Transformation: Embracing Innovation

The rise of Bitcoin prompts traditional banks to consider digital transformation. The blockchain technology underpinning Bitcoin has led to discussions within the banking sector about adopting distributed ledger technology (DLT) for more efficient and transparent financial processes.

6.   Competition and Collaboration: Shaping Alliances

Bitcoin introduces competition to traditional banking services, particularly in areas like international payments. Some banks respond by exploring collaborations with blockchain and cryptocurrency projects, seeking to leverage the benefits of this innovative technology while maintaining relevance in a changing financial landscape.

7.   Cryptocurrency Services: Integrating New Offerings

To stay competitive, some traditional banks are integrating cryptocurrency services. This may include offering cryptocurrency custody services, allowing clients to hold and manage digital assets within traditional banking platforms.

8.   Regulatory Response: Shaping the Landscape

The emergence of Bitcoin has prompted regulatory responses globally. While some jurisdictions embrace and regulate cryptocurrency, others approach it cautiously or with skepticism. Regulatory decisions influence how traditional banks engage with Bitcoin, affecting the level of integration and services they can offer.

9.   Security Considerations: Balancing Risks and Rewards

The security features of Bitcoin transactions, rooted in blockchain technology, prompt traditional banks to reconsider their security protocols. While Bitcoin transactions are secure and transparent, the cryptographic nature of the technology demands that banks adapt to new security challenges and opportunities.

10. Customer Expectations: Evolving Demands

The increasing popularity of Bitcoin influences customer expectations. Users accustomed to the efficiency and accessibility of Bitcoin transactions may demand similar features from traditional banking services, pushing banks to innovate and enhance their offerings to meet evolving customer demands.

11. Financial Sovereignty: Empowering Individuals

Bitcoin's emphasis on financial sovereignty challenges the traditional banking narrative where individuals rely on banks as custodians of their funds. Bitcoin users have direct control over their private keys, questioning the need for traditional banking institutions as intermediaries in financial affairs.

12. Innovation Catalyst: Spurring Technological Advancements

The disruptive nature of Bitcoin serves as a catalyst for technological advancements within the financial sector. Traditional banks are increasingly exploring blockchain technology, smart contracts, and other innovations to enhance efficiency, reduce costs, and remain competitive in the evolving financial landscape.

In conclusion, the global impact of Bitcoin on traditional banking is multifaceted, ranging from challenges to established models to opportunities for collaboration and innovation. As the financial ecosystem continues to evolve, the relationship between Bitcoin and traditional banking will likely shape the future trajectory of the entire financial industry.

Chapter 4: Challenges Facing Bitcoin

While Bitcoin has emerged as a transformative force in the financial world, its journey is not without hurdles and challenges. In this chapter, we delve into the various obstacles and complexities that Bitcoin encounters, exploring the ongoing debates, technical limitations, and external factors that shape the narrative around the world's most prominent cryptocurrency.

1. Scalability Concerns: Navigating Transaction Volume

Bitcoin faces challenges related to scalability, particularly as transaction volumes increase. The limited block size and block time pose obstacles to handling a growing number of transactions efficiently. Solutions such as Segregated Witness (SegWit) and the Lightning Network aim to address these scalability concerns, but debates around implementation persist.

2. Energy Consumption Debate: Environmental Impact

The energy consumption associated with Bitcoin mining has sparked considerable debate. Critics raise concerns about its environmental impact, especially as the Proof-of-Work consensus mechanism requires substantial computational power. Ongoing discussions focus on mitigating environmental effects and exploring alternative consensus mechanisms.

3.   Regulatory Uncertainty: Navigating Legal Frameworks

Bitcoin operates in a regulatory landscape that varies globally. Uncertainties regarding legal status, taxation, and compliance requirements create challenges for businesses and users. Striking a balance between regulatory oversights and preserving the decentralized nature of Bitcoin remains an ongoing debate.

4.   Privacy Concerns: Balancing Transparency and Anonymity

While Bitcoin transactions are transparent and recorded on the blockchain, privacy concerns persist. The pseudonymous nature of transactions has led to debates about the balance between transparency and user privacy. Improving privacy features, such as through coin mixing and technologies like Confidential Transactions, is an ongoing area of development.

5.   Security Risks: External Threats and Attacks

Bitcoin's security model relies on the robustness of its network and the integrity of miners. While the network has demonstrated resilience, potential threats, including 51% attacks and vulnerabilities in wallet software, underscore the importance of ongoing vigilance and collaborative efforts within the Bitcoin community.

6. Volatility: Impacts on Adoption and Everyday Use

Bitcoin's price volatility presents challenges for its adoption as a medium of exchange. Merchants and users may be hesitant to use Bitcoin for everyday transactions due to concerns about price fluctuations. Stablecoin projects and layer-2 solutions aim to address this issue, fostering a more stable ecosystem.

7. Technological Innovation: Balancing Tradition and Evolution

As Bitcoin evolves, debates arise about the balance between preserving its core principles and embracing technological innovations. Introducing new features or protocols requires community consensus, and finding common ground amid diverse perspectives is an ongoing challenge.

8. User Education: Promoting Understanding and Security

The complexity of Bitcoin and its underlying technology poses challenges for user education. Promoting a deeper understanding of private key management, security best practices, and the intricacies of the cryptocurrency space is crucial for enhancing user confidence and reducing risks.

9. Interoperability: Bridging Blockchain Networks

Bitcoin exists within a broader blockchain ecosystem, and achieving interoperability between different blockchain networks remains a challenge. Efforts to facilitate seamless interactions between Bitcoin and other decentralized platforms aim to enhance the overall functionality of the cryptocurrency space.

10. Community Governance: Navigating Decentralized Decision-Making

Decentralized governance is a cornerstone of Bitcoin's ethos, but reaching consensus on protocol upgrades and changes poses challenges. Debates around network upgrades, as seen in past events like the Bitcoin scaling debate, highlight the complexities of decentralized decision-making within the community.

11. Institutional Adoption: Balancing Integration and Autonomy

As institutional interest in Bitcoin grows, finding a balance between integration into traditional financial systems and preserving the decentralized ethos is a challenge. Discussions around Bitcoin exchange-traded funds (ETFs), institutional custody solutions, and regulatory compliance underscore the delicate balance between mainstream adoption and decentralization.

12. Cultural Perception: Shaping Public Trust and Understanding

Public perception of Bitcoin is influenced by cultural narratives, media coverage, and evolving societal attitudes. Overcoming misconceptions, fostering positive narratives, and promoting a nuanced understanding of

Bitcoin's potential and challenges are ongoing efforts within the cryptocurrency community.

In navigating these challenges, the Bitcoin ecosystem continues to evolve, driven by the collaborative efforts of developers, users, and stakeholders. While these obstacles pose complexities, they also represent opportunities for innovation, resilience, and the ongoing refinement of Bitcoin as a revolutionary force in the global financial landscape.

4.1 Scalability Issues

Scalability stands as a central challenge in the ongoing development and adoption of Bitcoin, impacting the network's ability to handle an increasing number of transactions efficiently. Several key scalability issues have emerged, prompting the exploration of innovative solutions within the Bitcoin community.

1. **Limited Block Size: Transaction Throughput Constraint**

Bitcoin's block size is capped, currently at 1 megabyte (MB) per block. This limitation restricts the number of transactions that can be included in each block, leading to congestion during periods of high demand. As a result, users may experience delays and increased fees, hindering the scalability of the network.

2. **Block Time: 10-Minute Confirmation Delays**

Bitcoin's block time, set at 10 minutes, contributes to transaction confirmation delays. While this interval ensures network security, it can lead to longer confirmation times, especially during periods of high transaction volume. Users may find this delay problematic, particularly in contexts where faster transaction processing is essential.

3. Transaction Fees: Escalating Costs During Congestion

As the demand for block space increases, transaction fees rise as users compete to have their transactions included in the limited block size. This fee market dynamics, while serving as an incentive for miners, can result in users paying higher fees during peak periods, affecting the cost-effectiveness of using Bitcoin for transactions.

4. Segregated Witness (SegWit): Alleviating Block Size Constraints

Segregated Witness, or SegWit, is a protocol upgrade implemented to address scalability concerns. By segregating signature data from transaction data, SegWit increases the effective block size, allowing for more transactions to be included in a block. While widely adopted, its impact on overall scalability remains a topic of ongoing discussion.

5. Lightning Network: Off-Chain Scalability Solution

The Lightning Network is a layer-2 scaling solution designed to facilitate faster and cheaper transactions off-chain. By creating payment channels between users, the Lightning Network aims to reduce the burden on the main blockchain. While it shows promise, widespread adoption and ongoing development are necessary for its full scalability potential to be realized.

6. Decentralization vs. Scalability: Striking a Balance

Maintaining decentralization is a core tenet of Bitcoin's philosophy. However, scalability solutions often introduce trade-offs that impact decentralization. Striking the right balance between scaling the network to accommodate increased demand and preserving its decentralized nature remains a complex challenge.

7. Network Node Requirements: Resource Intensiveness

Running a full Bitcoin node, essential for network security and decentralization, requires significant computational resources and storage space. As the blockchain grows, these requirements increase, potentially limiting the ability of individual users to participate in maintaining the network.

8. Security Considerations: Avoiding Compromises

Scalability solutions must navigate security considerations to prevent vulnerabilities and compromises. Changes to the protocol or the introduction of new technologies should undergo rigorous testing to ensure that they do not compromise the security and integrity of the Bitcoin network.

9. Consensus Challenges: Achieving Community Agreement

Implementing scalability solutions requires consensus within the Bitcoin community. Achieving agreement among diverse stakeholders with differing perspectives on how to address scalability challenges can be a protracted process, slowing down the implementation of necessary upgrades.

10. Evolutionary Nature: Adapting to Changing Demands

Bitcoin's scalability challenges are dynamic and must be addressed in an evolving landscape. As the cryptocurrency space continues to grow and user demands change, ongoing innovations and adaptations are essential to ensure that Bitcoin remains a scalable and viable decentralized currency.

In navigating these scalability issues, the Bitcoin community remains engaged in ongoing research, development, and collaborative efforts. As the network evolves, addressing scalability challenges is pivotal to realizing Bitcoin's full potential as a global, decentralized, and scalable digital currency.

4.2 Security Concerns

Bitcoin's decentralized and open-source nature has provided a robust foundation for financial transactions and decentralized trust. However, the cryptocurrency faces various security concerns that require ongoing attention from the community. Understanding and addressing these concerns is crucial for maintaining the integrity and trustworthiness of the Bitcoin network.

1. **51% Attacks: Threat to Consensus**

A 51% attack occurs when an entity gains control of more than 50% of the network's mining power. With majority control, this entity could potentially manipulate transactions, double-spend, or prevent new transactions from being confirmed. The decentralized nature of Bitcoin relies on distributed consensus, making the prevention of 51% attacks a paramount concern.

2. **Double-Spending: Ensuring Transaction Integrity**

Double-spending is a potential risk where a user spends the same Bitcoin more than once. While the Bitcoin network is designed to prevent double-spending through its consensus mechanism, the possibility exists in certain scenarios, such as during network forks or attacks.

3.   Wallet Security: Protecting Private Keys

The security of Bitcoin holdings depends on the protection of private keys. Wallets, whether hardware, software, or paper, are vulnerable to theft, malware, or phishing attacks. Users must prioritize secure storage and backup procedures to prevent unauthorized access to their private keys.

4.   Exchange Vulnerabilities: Risks of Centralization

Centralized exchanges pose security risks as they act as custodians of users' funds. Incidents of hacking or internal fraud can lead to the loss of significant amounts of Bitcoin. The decentralized ethos of Bitcoin emphasizes the importance of secure, user-controlled storage rather than relying on centralized entities.

5.   Smart Contract Risks: Code Vulnerabilities

While Bitcoin's primary focus is on peer-to-peer transactions, the introduction of smart contracts on layer-2 solutions or sidechains introduces additional complexities. Smart contract vulnerabilities can potentially lead to exploits or unintended consequences, requiring thorough code auditing and testing.

6.   Privacy Concerns: Balancing Transparency

Bitcoin transactions are transparent and recorded on the public blockchain. While this transparency enhances accountability, it also raises privacy concerns. Techniques like coin mixing and privacy-focused protocols aim to provide users with increased privacy options.

7. Social Engineering: Human Factor Vulnerabilities

Users can be susceptible to social engineering attacks, where malicious actors exploit human psychology to gain unauthorized access to funds. Phishing attempts, fraudulent schemes, and impersonation can compromise the security of individuals who may unwittingly disclose sensitive information.

8. Regulatory Risks: Navigating Legal Frameworks

Uncertainties in regulatory environments globally can impact the security of Bitcoin-related businesses and users. Adhering to evolving legal requirements while preserving the decentralized nature of Bitcoin is a delicate balance that requires ongoing attention.

9. Network Upgrades: Ensuring Smooth Transitions

Consensus-driven upgrades to the Bitcoin protocol are necessary for improving security and functionality. However, achieving community consensus and executing upgrades smoothly without disruptions or forks requires careful coordination and communication.

10. Quantum Computing Threat: Future Considerations

While quantum computing remains in the realm of theoretical threats, it poses a potential risk to existing cryptographic algorithms, including those used in Bitcoin. Preparing for future advancements in quantum computing by exploring quantum-resistant cryptographic solutions is a proactive security measure.

11. Educational Awareness: Mitigating User Risks

The security of Bitcoin is closely tied to user knowledge and awareness. Educating users about best practices, potential risks, and security measures is essential for minimizing vulnerabilities stemming from common pitfalls and misunderstandings.

12. Interoperability Challenges: Bridging Diverse Ecosystems

As Bitcoin interacts with various blockchain ecosystems and emerging technologies, ensuring secure interoperability becomes crucial. Efforts to integrate Bitcoin with layer-2 solutions, decentralized finance (DeFi), and other innovations must prioritize security to prevent unintended vulnerabilities.

Addressing these security concerns requires a collaborative effort from the Bitcoin community, developers, regulators, and users. As Bitcoin continues to evolve, a commitment to ongoing research, education, and the implementation of robust security measures is vital to safeguard the integrity and trustworthiness of the world's first decentralized cryptocurrency.

4.3 Environmental Impact

Bitcoin's remarkable rise as a decentralized digital currency has brought to the forefront discussions about its environmental impact. As a cryptocurrency operating on a Proof-of-Work (PoW) consensus mechanism, Bitcoin mining requires substantial computational power, leading to both critiques and efforts within the community to address its environmental footprint.

1. **Energy Consumption: PoW Mining Intensity**

Bitcoin mining involves solving complex mathematical puzzles through PoW, a process that demands significant computational power. This has led to concerns about the high energy consumption associated with mining activities. Estimates vary, but some argue that the energy usage of the Bitcoin network is comparable to that of certain small nations.

2. **Carbon Footprint: Environmental Concerns**

The carbon footprint of Bitcoin mining is a key aspect of its environmental impact. The reliance on fossil fuels in regions where mining operations are prevalent contributes to greenhouse gas emissions. Critics argue that such emissions contradict global efforts to mitigate climate change.

3.   Renewable Energy Integration: Shifting Narratives

Efforts are underway to address environmental concerns by promoting the use of renewable energy in Bitcoin mining. Some mining operations are strategically located near renewable energy sources such as hydroelectric plants or utilize excess energy from renewable projects. The shift towards renewable energy is seen as a positive step in mitigating the environmental impact of Bitcoin.

4.   Energy Mix Transparency: Promoting Accountability

Calls for transparency in disclosing the energy mix used in Bitcoin mining have gained traction. Mining operations providing clear information about the sources of their energy contribute to a more accountable and informed discussion about the environmental impact of Bitcoin.

5.   Evolving Technologies: PoW Alternatives

The Bitcoin community is exploring alternative consensus mechanisms that are less energy-intensive than PoW. Proof-of-Stake (PoS) and other emerging technologies aim to maintain security while minimizing the environmental impact. However, transitioning to new consensus mechanisms requires careful consideration and community consensus.

6. Debates on Significance: Relative Impact Assessment

Discussions around the significance of Bitcoin's environmental impact often involve comparing it to traditional financial systems, gold mining, or other industries. While some argue that Bitcoin's impact is relatively small, others emphasize the importance of addressing environmental concerns regardless of scale.

7. Economic Benefits: Weighing Positive Contributions

Proponents argue that Bitcoin's economic benefits, such as financial inclusion, decentralization, and potential to disrupt traditional banking, should be considered alongside its environmental impact. Balancing the positive contributions with environmental concerns is crucial in shaping a comprehensive perspective.

8. Innovation for Efficiency: Optimizing Mining Practices

Ongoing innovations in mining hardware and techniques aim to enhance energy efficiency. These improvements, including the development of more energy-efficient ASIC (Application-Specific Integrated Circuit) miners, demonstrate a commitment to optimizing mining practices and mitigating the environmental impact of Bitcoin.

9. Global Distribution: Varied Environmental Impact

The environmental impact of Bitcoin mining varies globally due to differences in energy sources, regulations, and mining practices. Some regions heavily rely on coal, contributing to higher carbon footprints, while others leverage cleaner energy sources.

10. Long-Term Sustainability: Balancing Growth and Impact

Ensuring the long-term sustainability of Bitcoin requires a balanced approach that considers its growth trajectory alongside environmental impact. Collaborative efforts within the community and engagement with environmental stakeholders are essential to navigate this delicate balance.

As the cryptocurrency landscape evolves, ongoing discussions and innovations within the Bitcoin community will shape its environmental impact. Striking a balance between fostering a decentralized financial system and addressing environmental concerns is a complex task that requires the collective efforts of developers, miners, regulators, and the broader community.

Chapter 5: Societal Impact

As Bitcoin continues to permeate the global financial landscape, its societal impact becomes increasingly pronounced. This chapter delves into the multifaceted ways in which Bitcoin influences societies, exploring its implications on financial systems, individual empowerment, and broader socio-economic dynamics.

1.   Financial Inclusion: Empowering the Unbanked

Bitcoin's decentralized nature provides individuals without access to traditional banking systems an alternative means of financial inclusion. Through Bitcoin wallets on mobile devices, people in underserved regions can participate in the global economy, transact, and store value independently.

2.   Reducing Remittance Costs: Empowering Migrant Workers

Bitcoin's borderless nature facilitates cost-effective cross-border transactions, particularly benefiting migrant workers who rely on remittances. By reducing transaction fees and processing times, Bitcoin empowers individuals to send and receive funds more efficiently, contributing to financial resilience in migrant communities.

3.   Economic Sovereignty: Individual Empowerment

Bitcoin's emphasis on ownership of private keys grants users a level of economic sovereignty unparalleled in traditional financial systems. This empowerment allows individuals to have direct control over their funds, reducing dependence on centralized financial institutions.

4. Wealth Redistribution: Bridging Economic Disparities

Bitcoin's decentralized nature can contribute to wealth redistribution by providing individuals with opportunities for financial growth outside traditional banking systems. This potential for economic autonomy has the capacity to bridge economic disparities and empower those who may be marginalized in conventional financial structures.

5. Financial Education: Fostering Digital Literacy

The use of Bitcoin introduces opportunities for financial education and digital literacy. Understanding concepts such as private key management, blockchain technology, and decentralized finance (DeFi) encourages users to make informed financial decisions in the digital age.

6. Decentralization vs. Centralization: Shifting Power Dynamics

Bitcoin challenges the traditional power dynamics inherent in centralized financial systems. Operating on a decentralized network, reduces reliance on central authorities, fostering a shift in power toward individual users and the broader community.

7. Cultural Shift: Changing Attitudes toward Finance

The adoption of Bitcoin contributes to a cultural shift in how individuals perceive and engage with finance. It introduces concepts of decentralization, autonomy, and self-custody, challenging conventional notions of financial trust and control.

8. Entrepreneurship Opportunities: Unlocking Innovation

Bitcoin's decentralized and permissionless nature opens doors for entrepreneurial opportunities. Innovations in Bitcoin-related technologies, services, and applications provide a platform for entrepreneurial endeavors that can drive economic growth and creativity.

9. Privacy Advocacy: Empowering User Control

Bitcoin's pseudonymous transactions encourage privacy advocacy. While the public ledger records transactions, privacy-focused technologies, and methodologies allow users to exert greater control over the visibility of their financial activities.

10. Philanthropy and Aid: Direct Contributions

Bitcoin's use in philanthropy and aid allows for direct contributions to individuals in need. The decentralized nature of Bitcoin ensures that a larger portion of donations reaches recipients, bypassing traditional channels and potentially increasing the efficiency of charitable initiatives.

11. Challenges of Adoption: Navigating Cultural Barriers

The societal impact of Bitcoin is not without challenges. Cultural resistance, regulatory uncertainties, and a lack of understanding pose barriers to widespread adoption. Bridging these gaps requires educational efforts, regulatory clarity, and community engagement.

12. Global Perspectives: Diverse Interpretations

The societal impact of Bitcoin varies across cultures and regions. While some societies embrace the potential for financial autonomy and inclusion, others may approach Bitcoin with skepticism. Understanding and respecting diverse perspectives is crucial for fostering positive societal outcomes.

As Bitcoin's influence continues to unfold, its societal impact intertwines with ongoing discussions about financial autonomy, inclusivity, and the redefinition of traditional financial paradigms. This chapter provides a glimpse into the transformative potential of Bitcoin in shaping the socio-economic landscape on a global scale.

5.1 Changing Financial Paradigms with Bitcoin

Bitcoin, as a decentralized digital currency, is at the forefront of changing traditional financial paradigms. Its disruptive nature challenges long-standing conventions, reshaping how individuals, institutions, and societies perceive and interact with money. This section explores the transformative impact of Bitcoin on financial paradigms.

1. Decentralization: Redefining Trust in Finance

Bitcoin's decentralized nature challenges the traditional model of centralized financial control. By operating on a peer-to-peer network without reliance on intermediaries, it redefines trust in finance. Users gain direct control over their funds, reducing dependence on traditional banking institutions.

2. Financial Inclusion: Beyond Banking Boundaries

Bitcoin extends financial inclusion beyond the boundaries of traditional banking systems. Its decentralized network allows individuals without access to banking infrastructure to participate in global transactions, store value, and engage in economic activities independently.

3. Ownership and Control: Empowering Individuals

Bitcoin empowers individuals by emphasizing ownership and control over one's finances. The possession of private keys grants users exclusive control, challenging the conventional paradigm where banks act as custodians. This shift towards individual empowerment is central to changing financial dynamics.

4.   Global Transactions: Borderless Commerce

The borderless nature of Bitcoin transactions challenges the traditional constraints of international commerce. Businesses and individuals can engage in cross-border transactions without the need for intermediary banks, reducing costs and streamlining global trade.

5.   Digital Literacy: Fostering Financial Education

The use of Bitcoin fosters digital literacy and financial education. Concepts such as private key management, blockchain technology, and decentralized finance (DeFi) become integral components of financial literacy, empowering users to navigate the complexities of the digital financial landscape.

6.   Privacy Advocacy: Balancing Transparency and Anonymity

Bitcoin advocates for privacy in financial transactions while maintaining transparency through its public ledger. This shift challenges the traditional paradigm where financial activities are often subject to extensive surveillance. Users can control the visibility of their transactions, fostering a nuanced approach to financial privacy.

7.   Smart Contracts: Automating Financial Agreements

Bitcoin's programmable nature through smart contracts introduces automation to financial agreements. While not as extensive as some other blockchain platforms, Bitcoin's ability to execute self-executing contracts has the potential to streamline and innovate various financial processes.

8. Decentralized Finance (DeFi): Democratizing Services

The emergence of DeFi applications on the Bitcoin blockchain contributes to democratizing financial services. Individuals can access lending, borrowing, and other financial services without relying on traditional intermediaries, challenging the conventional banking model.

9. Store of Value: Redefining Asset Preservation

Bitcoin's narrative as a "digital gold" challenges traditional notions of asset preservation. Investors increasingly view Bitcoin as a store of value, diversifying portfolios and reconsidering the historical reliance on precious metals and traditional financial instruments.

10. Monetary Policy Innovation: Deflationary Model

Bitcoin's capped supply introduces a deflationary economic model, challenging the inflationary nature of traditional fiat currencies. This innovation prompts discussions about the long-term impact on monetary policy and economic stability.

11. Microtransactions: Facilitating Small-Scale Transactions

Bitcoin's divisibility allows for microtransactions, challenging the traditional paradigm where small-scale transactions may be hindered by high fees or impracticality. This feature opens avenues for innovative business models and supports economic activities on a smaller scale.

12. Community-Led Governance: Participatory Decision-Making

Bitcoin's community-led governance challenges the centralized decision-making typical of traditional financial institutions. Upgrades and changes to the protocol require consensus within the community, embodying a more participatory and decentralized approach to governance.

As Bitcoin continues to evolve, its transformative impact on financial paradigms unfolds. The decentralized, transparent, and inclusive nature of Bitcoin challenges traditional financial structures, paving the way for a more dynamic and user-centric financial landscape.

5.2 Empowering Individuals

Bitcoin, as a decentralized digital currency, stands as a powerful tool for empowering individuals in various aspects of their financial lives. From financial autonomy to privacy and inclusion, Bitcoin's impact extends beyond traditional paradigms, placing control back into the hands of users.

1. **Financial Sovereignty: Direct Ownership and Control**

Bitcoin empowers individuals by offering a level of financial sovereignty that is unparalleled in traditional systems. The ownership of private keys grants users direct control over their funds, eliminating the need for reliance on centralized institutions. This shift puts individuals in command of their financial destinies.

2. **Inclusive Access: Bridging the Unbanked Gap**

One of Bitcoin's most profound impacts is its ability to provide inclusive financial access. For the unbanked and underbanked populations, especially in regions with limited banking infrastructure, Bitcoin offers a gateway to participate in the global economy. All that's needed is a smartphone and internet access.

3. **Reducing Remittance Costs: Empowering Migrant Workers**

Bitcoin serves as a powerful tool for migrant workers, reducing the costs and inefficiencies associated with cross-border remittances. By cutting out intermediaries and enabling peer-to-peer transactions, Bitcoin empowers these individuals to send and receive funds more efficiently, preserving more of their hard-earned money.

4. **Financial Inclusion for the Marginalized**

Bitcoin has the potential to uplift marginalized communities that have historically faced challenges in accessing traditional banking services. The decentralized nature of Bitcoin allows individuals to become their own banks, fostering financial inclusion for those who may have been excluded from traditional financial systems.

5. Privacy and Security: Taking Control of Personal Data

Bitcoin transactions, based on cryptographic principles, provide a level of privacy and security that empowers users to control their personal financial data. Unlike traditional banking systems, where transactions are often subject to extensive surveillance, Bitcoin allows users to transact pseudonymously, enhancing financial privacy.

6. Ownership of Digital Assets: Democratizing Investments

Bitcoin enables individuals to become owners of digital assets, democratizing the investment landscape. Fractional ownership allows even those with modest resources to participate in the potential appreciation of Bitcoin, challenging the traditional model where investment opportunities were often reserved for the affluent.

7. Financial Education: Empowering Through Knowledge

Engaging with Bitcoin necessitates a certain level of financial education. As individuals learn about concepts like private key management, blockchain technology, and the importance of self-custody, they become more financially literate. This knowledge empowers users to navigate the complexities of the digital financial ecosystem.

8. Entrepreneurship Opportunities: Innovation and Creativity

Bitcoin's decentralized and permissionless nature opens avenues for entrepreneurial endeavors. From developing Bitcoin-related technologies to creating new financial services, individuals have the opportunity to innovate and contribute to the growing ecosystem, fostering entrepreneurship and creativity.

9. Crisis Resistance: Preserving Value in Uncertain Times

Bitcoin serves as a hedge against economic uncertainties and crises. In regions experiencing hyperinflation or currency devaluation, individuals can turn to Bitcoin to preserve the value of their assets, providing a means of empowerment during challenging economic conditions.

10. Community-Led Governance: Participatory Decision-Making

Bitcoin's governance structure relies on community participation and consensus. Individuals who engage with the Bitcoin network have the opportunity to contribute to decision-making processes, emphasizing a participatory approach that empowers users to shape the future of the cryptocurrency.

In conclusion, Bitcoin's empowerment of individuals extends far beyond financial transactions. It encompasses ownership, privacy, education, and the potential for economic self-determination. As Bitcoin continues to evolve, its impact on empowering individuals in the realm of finance is poised to play a pivotal role in shaping the future of decentralized economies.

5.3 Cultural Perspectives on Bitcoin

Bitcoin, as a global phenomenon, is not just a financial instrument but a cultural force that shapes and is shaped by diverse societies around the world. Cultural perspectives on Bitcoin vary widely, reflecting the unique values, beliefs, and economic contexts of different communities.

1. **Digital Revolution and Technological Optimism**

In some cultures, Bitcoin is embraced as a symbol of the digital revolution and technological optimism. It represents a departure from traditional financial systems and an entry into a new era of decentralized, borderless, and permissionless transactions, resonating with the values of innovation and progress.

2. **Financial Inclusion and Economic Empowerment**

Cultures that experience limited access to traditional banking systems often view Bitcoin as a tool for financial inclusion and economic empowerment. The ability to transact globally without relying on intermediaries aligns with the cultural narrative of autonomy and self-sufficiency.

3.   Skepticism and Traditionalism

Conversely, some cultures approach Bitcoin with skepticism, rooted in a strong attachment to traditional financial structures. The idea of decentralized currency may clash with established norms and values, leading to apprehension or resistance to adopting Bitcoin as a legitimate form of value.

4.   Speculation and Investment Culture

In cultures with a strong investment culture, Bitcoin is often viewed through the lens of speculation and potential wealth accumulation. The volatility of Bitcoin's price, coupled with stories of early adopters benefiting from substantial gains, attracts individuals looking to participate in speculative investment opportunities.

5.   Privacy Concerns and Cultural Values

Cultural values related to privacy influence perspectives on Bitcoin, especially in regions where financial transactions are considered highly private matters. Bitcoin's pseudonymous transactions provide a balance between transparency and privacy, aligning with cultural expectations regarding financial confidentiality.

6. Resistance to Change and Regulatory Concerns

Cultures that resist rapid changes or have strong regulatory frameworks may express concerns about Bitcoin's impact on existing financial structures. Regulatory uncertainties, perceived risks, and fears of financial instability can influence cultural perspectives on the adoption and acceptance of Bitcoin.

7. Digital Literacy and Education

Cultural attitudes toward education and digital literacy play a significant role in shaping perspectives on Bitcoin. Societies with a strong emphasis on education may be more open to understanding the complexities of blockchain technology, smart contracts, and the potential societal impacts of decentralized finance.

8. Entrepreneurial Spirit and Innovation

Cultures with a strong entrepreneurial spirit often view Bitcoin as a platform for innovation and new business opportunities. Bitcoin's permissionless nature allows for the development of diverse applications and services, aligning with cultural values that encourage creativity and entrepreneurship.

9.   Community and Social Movement

Bitcoin has become more than just a currency; it's a social movement for some cultures. Communities that share common values of decentralization, censorship resistance, and financial autonomy rally around Bitcoin as a symbol of collective empowerment and a tool for challenging established norms.

10.   Philanthropy and Social Impact

Cultural perspectives on Bitcoin may also involve its potential for philanthropy and social impact. Bitcoin's use in charitable donations, disaster relief, and community-driven initiatives aligns with cultural values of altruism and community support.

11.   Symbol of Rebellion and Dissent

In cultures where individuals feel disenfranchised or dissatisfied with centralized authority, Bitcoin can be seen as a symbol of rebellion and dissent. Its decentralized nature appeals to those seeking alternatives to traditional financial systems and questioning established power structures.

12.   Cultural Narratives in Media and Art

Media and art play a crucial role in shaping cultural narratives around Bitcoin. Whether portrayed as a disruptor, a tool for liberation, or a risky venture, cultural representations in literature, films, and visual arts contribute to how Bitcoin is perceived within a given society.

Understanding these diverse cultural perspectives on Bitcoin is essential for comprehending its global impact. As Bitcoin continues to evolve, its reception within different cultural contexts will shape and be shaped by the complex interplay of values, beliefs, and societal dynamics.

Chapter 6: Future Outlook

The future of Bitcoin holds both promise and intrigue as this decentralized digital currency continues to evolve amid technological advancements, regulatory developments, and shifting global perspectives. This chapter delves into the potential trajectories, challenges, and transformative possibilities that may shape the future of Bitcoin.

1. Technological Advancements: Innovating Beyond the Horizon

Bitcoin's underlying technology, blockchain, is subject to continuous innovation. Technological advancements such as scalability solutions, layer-2 protocols, and improvements in privacy features are likely to enhance the efficiency and usability of the Bitcoin network.

2. Evolving Regulatory Landscape: Navigating Legal Frontiers

The regulatory environment plays a pivotal role in shaping Bitcoin's future. As governments and regulatory bodies worldwide grapple with the classification and oversight of cryptocurrencies, a clearer regulatory framework may emerge, providing both legitimacy and guidelines for the industry.

3.   Institutional Adoption: Mainstream Integration

The increasing involvement of institutional players in the cryptocurrency space is a trend poised to continue. Institutional adoption of Bitcoin as an asset class, investment vehicle, or part of corporate treasuries could contribute to its mainstream acceptance and integration into traditional financial systems.

4.   Decentralized Finance (DeFi): Shaping Financial Paradigms

The rise of decentralized finance (DeFi) ecosystems built on the Bitcoin blockchain or layer-2 solutions may redefine traditional financial services. Smart contracts, lending protocols, and decentralized exchanges could transform how individuals interact with financial instruments, offering new avenues for financial empowerment.

5.   Privacy Enhancements: Balancing Transparency and Anonymity

As privacy concerns gain prominence, the development of privacy-focused technologies within the Bitcoin ecosystem is likely to intensify. Solutions like Confidential Transactions and CoinJoin implementations could provide users with enhanced privacy options, striking a balance between transparency and anonymity.

6. Global Economic Uncertainties: Bitcoin as a Safe Haven

Bitcoin's role as a store of value and a hedge against economic uncertainties may amplify in the face of global economic challenges. Factors such as inflation, currency devaluation, and geopolitical tensions could drive increased adoption of Bitcoin as a means of preserving wealth.

7. Layer-2 Scaling Solutions: Improving Transaction Efficiency

Scalability challenges have prompted the development and adoption of layer-2 scaling solutions. Technologies like the Lightning Network aim to facilitate faster and more cost-effective transactions off-chain, addressing concerns related to transaction throughput and fees.

8. Community-Led Development: Decentralized Governance in Action

The decentralized nature of Bitcoin's development and governance may continue to play a crucial role. Community-driven initiatives, open-source contributions, and grassroots efforts are likely to shape the evolution of Bitcoin, emphasizing the importance of consensus among diverse stakeholders.

9. **Technological Interoperability: Bridging Blockchain Ecosystems**

As the broader blockchain space evolves, the need for interoperability between different blockchain ecosystems becomes evident. Efforts to facilitate seamless interactions between Bitcoin and other blockchain platforms may lead to innovative cross-chain solutions.

10. **Educational Initiatives: Fostering Understanding and Adoption**

Education will remain a key factor in shaping the future of Bitcoin. Increased efforts to educate individuals, businesses, and policymakers about the benefits, risks, and mechanisms of Bitcoin could contribute to a more informed and receptive global community.

11. **Environmental Sustainability: Exploring Green Solutions**

Addressing concerns about the environmental impact of Bitcoin mining may drive the exploration of more sustainable practices. The industry may witness a shift towards increased use of renewable energy sources, energy-efficient mining technologies, and a broader commitment to environmental responsibility.

12. Cultural Integration: Adapting to Diverse Perspectives

Bitcoin's integration into diverse cultural contexts will influence its trajectory. Cultural acceptance, regulatory approaches, and local economic conditions will play a pivotal role in determining the level of adoption and use of Bitcoin in different societies.

The future of Bitcoin is a dynamic interplay of technological innovation, regulatory developments, and societal acceptance. As the landscape continues to evolve, the decentralized ethos of Bitcoin, coupled with its potential to reshape financial paradigms, positions it as a transformative force with enduring global implications. The unfolding chapters of Bitcoin's journey hold the promise of a decentralized future that reshapes the way we perceive and engage with finance on a global scale.

6.1 Evolution of Bitcoin Technology

The journey of Bitcoin is a testament to the continuous evolution of its underlying technology. From its inception in 2009 by the pseudonymous creator Satoshi Nakamoto to the present day, Bitcoin has undergone significant advancements and adaptations. This evolution encompasses various aspects, including the core protocol, scalability solutions, privacy enhancements, and the broader ecosystem surrounding this pioneering cryptocurrency.

1. Genesis of Bitcoin: Birth of a Decentralized Vision (2009-2010)

The story begins with the release of the Bitcoin software in 2009, introducing a decentralized, and peer-to-peer electronic cash system.

The foundational technology included the blockchain, a public ledger recording all transactions. Early adopters mined new bitcoins using Proof-of-Work (PoW), establishing the first blocks of the chain.

2. Early Improvements: Introduction of Version 0.1 to 0.3 (2010-2012)

The initial versions of the Bitcoin software laid the groundwork for subsequent improvements. Version 0.3, released in 2010, introduced a more user-friendly interface. During this period, the community grew, and exchanges emerged, facilitating the first real-world transactions using Bitcoin.

3. Transition to Version 0.8: Blockchain Forks and Client Diversity (2012-2013)

The Bitcoin software experienced forks in the blockchain due to incompatible rule changes, leading to the introduction of version 0.8. This version emphasized performance improvements and marked the beginning of a diverse ecosystem of Bitcoin clients, reducing reliance on a single implementation.

4. Scaling Debate: Segregated Witness (SegWit) Activation (2017)

The scalability debate reached a pivotal moment in 2017 with the activation of Segregated Witness (SegWit). This upgrade aimed to increase the block size limit and enable the implementation of second-layer scaling solutions, addressing concerns about transaction throughput and fees.

5. Emergence of the Lightning Network (2018-Present)

The Lightning Network, a second-layer scaling solution, gained prominence in addressing Bitcoin's scalability challenges. Introduced as a payment protocol built on top of the Bitcoin blockchain, it enables faster and more cost-effective transactions by conducting them off-chain, fostering microtransactions and scalability.

6. Privacy Enhancements: Confidential Transactions and Schnorr Signatures (2019-Present)

Privacy considerations led to the exploration of Confidential Transactions, enhancing transaction privacy by hiding transaction amounts. Ongoing developments include the integration of Schnorr Signatures, a cryptographic innovation that enables more efficient and private multi-signature transactions.

7. Taproot Activation: Smart Contracts and Scripting Upgrades (2021)

Taproot, activated in 2021, represents a significant upgrade to Bitcoin's scripting capabilities. This improvement enhances privacy and enables the implementation of more complex smart contracts. It also streamlines the use of multi-signature wallets, making them more indistinguishable from regular transactions.

8.   Environmental Sustainability Initiatives (Ongoing)

Concerns about the environmental impact of Bitcoin mining have prompted initiatives to explore more sustainable practices. From the adoption of renewable energy sources to the development of energy-efficient mining technologies, the industry is actively working towards minimizing its ecological footprint.

9.   Layer-2 Solutions and Sidechains (Ongoing)

Ongoing efforts focus on further scalability through Layer-2 solutions and sidechains. Technologies like the Liquid Network and other innovative approaches aim to enable faster, more efficient transactions while maintaining the security and decentralization of the Bitcoin network.

10. Continued Research and Development (Ongoing)

Bitcoin's evolution remains an ongoing process with a vibrant community of developers, researchers, and contributors. Continuous research and development initiatives explore new technologies, improvements to consensus mechanisms, and ways to enhance the overall resilience and functionality of the Bitcoin network.

The evolution of Bitcoin technology reflects a commitment to addressing challenges, embracing innovation, and maintaining the core principles of decentralization and security. As the cryptocurrency landscape continues to mature, Bitcoin stands as a resilient and continuously evolving force at the forefront of decentralized finance.

6.2 Potential Integrations

Bitcoin's versatility and decentralized nature open the door to a myriad of potential integrations across various sectors. As the cryptocurrency ecosystem evolves, innovative applications and use cases emerge, showcasing the adaptability of Bitcoin. Here are some potential integrations that could further expand the reach and impact of Bitcoin:

1. **Cross-Border Payments and Remittances**

Bitcoin's borderless nature makes it an ideal solution for facilitating cross-border payments and remittances. Integrating Bitcoin into existing financial infrastructures can lead to faster, cost-effective, and inclusive international transactions, particularly in regions with limited access to traditional banking services.

2. **Retail and E-Commerce**

As an accepted form of payment, Bitcoin could streamline transactions in the retail and e-commerce sectors. Integration with payment processors and platforms would enable consumers to make purchases using Bitcoin, fostering financial inclusivity and providing an alternative payment method.

3. Digital Identity and Authentication

The blockchain technology underlying Bitcoin can be leveraged for secure digital identity and authentication systems. Integration with identity verification platforms could enhance privacy and security, allowing users to control access to their personal information.

4. Smart Contracts and Decentralized Applications (DApps)

Bitcoin's integration with smart contract functionality could unlock a new realm of decentralized applications. Building DApps on the Bitcoin blockchain could offer innovative solutions in areas such as decentralized finance (DeFi), gaming, and supply chain management.

5. Microtransactions and Content Monetization

Bitcoin's divisibility allows for microtransactions, making it suitable for content monetization on platforms such as social media, blogs, and streaming services. Integrating Bitcoin for small payments could create new revenue streams for content creators while reducing transaction costs.

6.   Supply Chain and Provenance Tracking

Utilizing Bitcoin's transparent and immutable ledger, supply chains can integrate blockchain technology to track the provenance of products. This enhances transparency, reduces fraud, and provides consumers with verifiable information about the origin and authenticity of goods.

7.   Tokenization of Assets

Bitcoin's integration with tokenization platforms could enable the representation of real-world assets, such as real estate or art, as digital tokens on the blockchain. This could enhance liquidity, accessibility, and fractional ownership of traditionally illiquid assets.

8.   Education and Certification Verification

Bitcoin's blockchain can be utilized for secure and tamper-resistant verification of educational credentials and certifications. Integrating with educational institutions and certification bodies could streamline the verification process, reducing fraud and enhancing trust.

9.   Charitable Donations and Philanthropy

Bitcoin's use in charitable donations has already gained traction. Further integration with fundraising platforms could provide a transparent and efficient way for individuals and organizations to contribute to causes globally, with the added benefit of reducing transaction costs.

10. Energy and Sustainability Tracking

In response to environmental concerns, integrating Bitcoin with platforms that track energy consumption and sustainability efforts in mining could enhance transparency. This data could be used to promote eco-friendly mining practices and mitigate the environmental impact of Bitcoin.

11. Insurance and Risk Management

The transparency and immutability of blockchain can be applied to insurance and risk management. Integration with insurance platforms could streamline processes, reduce fraud, and enhance trust through transparent and verifiable records of policies and claims.

12. Real-Time Settlement in Financial Markets

Bitcoin's potential integration with traditional financial markets could facilitate real-time settlement of transactions. This could reduce counterparty risk, increase liquidity, and enhance the efficiency of financial market operations.

These potential integrations illustrate the diverse applications and transformative capabilities of Bitcoin beyond its role as a digital currency. As technology continues to advance and regulatory frameworks evolve, the integration of Bitcoin into various sectors has the potential to redefine how we transact, authenticate, and interact with digital assets in the modern era.

6.3 Shaping the Future of Finance

Bitcoin, as a decentralized digital currency, is poised to play a transformative role in shaping the future of finance. Its unique characteristics and underlying blockchain technology have the potential to revolutionize traditional financial systems, offering new possibilities and paving the way for a more inclusive, transparent, and efficient financial landscape.

1. Financial Inclusion: Bridging the Gap

Bitcoin has the power to extend financial services to the unbanked and underbanked populations globally. By providing a decentralized and borderless alternative, it can bridge the gap for individuals who lack access to traditional banking systems. Empowering the underserved with financial tools and inclusion is a crucial step toward creating a more equitable global economy.

2. Decentralization: Redefining Trust in Finance

The decentralized nature of Bitcoin challenges the traditional model of centralized financial control. By operating on a peer-to-peer network without intermediaries, it reduces reliance on centralized authorities. This shift towards decentralization redefines trust in finance, placing greater control in the hands of individual users.

3.   Global Transactions: Breaking Down Borders

Bitcoin's borderless nature facilitates seamless and cost-effective cross-border transactions. Traditional financial systems are often hindered by lengthy processes and high fees for international transfers. Bitcoin's ability to transcend borders fosters a more interconnected global economy, enabling individuals and businesses to transact without the constraints of geographic boundaries.

4.   Ownership and Control: Empowering Individuals

Bitcoin emphasizes ownership and control over one's finances. The possession of private keys grants users exclusive control, reducing dependence on centralized financial institutions. This empowerment encourages a shift in financial dynamics, where individuals have direct control over their assets, fostering a sense of economic self-determination.

5.   Financial Privacy: Balancing Transparency and Anonymity

Bitcoin's pseudonymous transactions offer a balance between financial transparency and individual privacy. While transactions are recorded on the public ledger, users can control the visibility of their financial activities. This aspect challenges the conventional notion of complete financial transparency and advocates for individual privacy in the digital age.

6.   Smart Contracts and Programmable Money

The integration of smart contracts on the Bitcoin blockchain has the potential to revolutionize financial agreements. Programmable money allows for the execution of self-executing contracts without the need for intermediaries. This innovation opens avenues for more efficient, secure, and automated financial processes.

7.   Store of Value: Redefining Asset Preservation

Bitcoin's narrative as "digital gold" challenges traditional notions of asset preservation. Investors increasingly view Bitcoin as a store of value, diversifying portfolios and reconsidering historical reliance on precious metals and traditional financial instruments. This shift contributes to a reevaluation of traditional approaches to wealth preservation.

8.   Microtransactions and Financial Micropayments

Bitcoin's divisibility allows for microtransactions, enabling small-scale financial activities that were previously impractical or cost-prohibitive. This feature opens new possibilities for innovative business models, content monetization, and economic interactions on a smaller scale.

9. Blockchain-Based Governance: Decentralized Decision-Making

The use of blockchain for governance purposes can facilitate decentralized decision-making processes. Community-led governance in the Bitcoin network ensures that updates and changes require consensus among participants, fostering a more inclusive and participatory approach to financial system development.

10. Philanthropy and Aid: Direct Contributions

Bitcoin's use in philanthropy allows for direct contributions to individuals and causes in need. The decentralized and transparent nature of Bitcoin transactions ensures that a larger portion of donations reaches recipients, potentially increasing the efficiency and impact of charitable initiatives.

11. Entrepreneurship Opportunities: Fostering Innovation

Bitcoin's permissionless nature creates opportunities for entrepreneurship. Innovations in Bitcoin-related technologies, services, and applications contribute to economic growth and creativity. The decentralized ecosystem fosters an environment where individuals can explore entrepreneurial endeavors without traditional barriers.

12. Regulatory Adaptation: Navigating the Future

The evolving regulatory landscape will play a pivotal role in shaping the future of Bitcoin. Collaborative efforts between the cryptocurrency industry and regulatory authorities can lead to a clearer framework that balances innovation with consumer protection, providing the foundation for sustainable growth and mainstream acceptance.

In conclusion, Bitcoin is not just a digital currency; it is a catalyst for reimagining the future of finance. It's decentralized, transparent, and inclusive features challenge traditional financial paradigms, offering a glimpse into a future where financial systems prioritize individual empowerment, global connectivity, and innovative possibilities. As Bitcoin continues to evolve, its impact on shaping the future of finance is destined to be a driving force in the ongoing transformation of the global economic landscape.

Conclusion

In the journey through the pages of "Bitcoin: The Revolution of Decentralized Digital Currency and Understanding the Potential, Challenges, and Impact of the World's Most Disruptive Cryptocurrency," we have delved into the heart of a financial revolution that is reshaping the way we perceive, interact with, and understand money. Bitcoin, born out of the decentralized ethos and powered by blockchain technology, has emerged as a groundbreaking force with the potential to redefine the very fabric of global finance.

Unveiling the Potential:

Bitcoin's potential reaches far beyond its origins as a digital currency. It embodies a vision of financial inclusion, borderless transactions, and empowerment for individuals across the globe. The chapters unfolded the vast potential of Bitcoin:

- ***Financial Inclusion***: Providing access to financial services for the unbanked.
- ***Decentralization***: Redefining trust in financial systems.
- ***Global Transactions***: Breaking down geographical barriers.
- ***Ownership and Control***: Empowering individuals over their finances.
- ***Financial Privacy***: Balancing transparency with individual anonymity.

Navigating the Challenges:

Yet, the journey of Bitcoin is not without its challenges. Scalability issues, regulatory uncertainties, environmental concerns, and the need for continued technological advancements pose hurdles that the community strives to overcome. Addressing these challenges is integral to ensuring Bitcoin's sustainable growth and mainstream acceptance.

Embracing the Impact:

As we conclude, it is evident that the impact of Bitcoin extends beyond its role as a disruptor of traditional finance. The ripple effects are felt across diverse realms:

- ***Cultural Perspectives***: Shaping and being shaped by diverse societies.
- ***Technological Evolution***: Constantly adapting to scale, privacy, and efficiency.
- ***Financial Paradigms***: Challenging traditional norms and structures.
- ***Future Outlook***: Paving the way for a decentralized, interconnected future.
- ***Potential Integrations***: Transforming sectors beyond digital currency.

The Ongoing Evolution:

Bitcoin is not a static entity; it is a living, breathing force that evolves with each block, each transaction, and each challenge faced. Its decentralized governance, community-driven development, and resilience in the face of adversity showcase the strength of a network built on principles of transparency, security, and collaboration.

In our exploration of the Bitcoin revolution, we have witnessed a financial paradigm shift that goes beyond the realm of currency. It is a movement that champions financial sovereignty, inclusivity, and individual empowerment. As Bitcoin continues to navigate the uncharted waters of mainstream adoption and regulatory clarity, its journey remains a testament to the power of decentralized innovation.

The revolution is ongoing, and the potential is boundless. Whether you are a seasoned crypto enthusiast, a curious observer, or a skeptic cautiously eyeing the developments, the story of Bitcoin invites you to be part of a narrative that transcends individual transactions and embraces a vision of a more equitable, transparent, and interconnected financial future. As we turn the last page, let us carry forward the lessons learned and the possibilities envisioned, knowing that the Bitcoin revolution is not just a chapter in history but an ongoing saga that continues to unfold.